SLUT SHAMED

Inappropriate Feminist Poems

Poems from the Attic, Book Two

Alicia Bayer

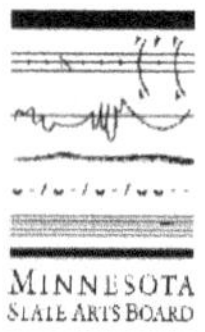

Alicia Bayer is a fiscal year 2021 recipient of a Creative Support for
Individuals grant from the Minnesota State Arts Board. This activity is
made possible by the voters of Minnesota through a grant from the
Minnesota State Arts Board, thanks to a legislative appropriation from the
arts and cultural heritage fund.

For Polly,

who never learned how beautiful she is.

CONTENTS

Introduction 9

You're So Pretty 11

E.R. 13

DAY LILIES 14

UPON WAKING 15

ALLOUETTE 16

TEN THINGS MY DAUGHTER LEARNED FROM FAIRY TALES 18

NOT YOUR USUAL COSMO QUIZ 19

WHITE WALLS 22

SERVICE 24

You Know How Women Are 25

ENTITLED 27

PURGED 28

REFLECTIONS ON HANES 29

SHE THINKS SHE'S AN EAGLE 30

TARAXACUM OFFICINALIS 31

MASENGILL 32

BATHING THE NUDE SAVIOR 33

OH YES 34

And We Never Cry 37

FLOWERED 39

DANCING GIRL 40

CHANCES 42

NIGHTMARES 43

MOONCHILD 44

WATERGIRL 45

FASHION STATEMENT 46

THE SCORE 47

DIAMOND POINT 48

Closed Eyes 49

NECROPHILIA 51

WITNESS 52

INTRUDERS 53

A SONG FOR THE OTHER CHILDREN 54

SURVIVORS 55

DEPTH 56

LAURA MILLER'S EYES 58

THE OUTING 60

WHITE FEMALE 61

WINTER 62

6 YEARS TRAINING 63

When I Was Under Glass 65

THE WICKED WOMAN 67

TO HEAVEN 68

OFFER 69

BURNING LOVE 70

THE WAKE 71

THE PROBLEM WITH HEROES 72

ALONE AND DAHLIA 73

THE RIVER 74

DRIVE 75

So Often So Badly 77

ALL I WANT 79

ON BEING A WOMAN AND A POET 80

MENTOR 82

RIGHTS 83

BEST OF 84

THE PROCESS 86

THE PAGE 87

HIGH HOPES 88

What You Cannot Own 89

AUNT LINDA'S GHOST 91

WEDDING DAYS 94

SEVEN WITH PAROLE 96

WITCHES 98

EMPATHY IN C MINOR 100

BUTCHERED 102

DOMESTIC ABUSE 104

Those Evil Bitches 105

KOHL 107

HEDONISM 108

BLOOD LETTING 110

AMPU- TATIONS 111

BOUND 112

KANGAROO MOTHER 113

ESCAPISM 116

AZUCAR 114

EVER AFTER 115

Whether To Dream 116

MOON RUNNING 119

ONE GAME 122

IRISES 120

SILVER 121

SAINT JOSEPH'S 122

SOMEDAY 126

NOTHING WAS WASTED 126

THE PRINCE 128

Introduction

When I was fourteen years old, I decided to become a slut. I had no experience with boys (sexual abuse doesn't count) but I was tired of being known as a nerd, or worse, invisible, and men had taught me from an early age that my sexuality was my biggest worth. So I decided to cultivate a reputation. I was wildly successful. In the years that followed, I was the most notorious slut that Bemidji, Minnesota, had ever seen.

I moved every year of my childhood and when I started college in a new state at seventeen, I reinvented myself again. I was homeless, poor and a thousand miles from my only support system. Someone asked me to marry him. It was a way to survive. And so, at eighteen years old I became a wife.

I worked full time while going to school full time, cooking meals, doing laundry and putting out. I majored in creative writing and minored in Women's Studies, where feminism planted sneaky new seeds.

Five years into my marriage and back in Minnesota, my husband deemed me "too fucking crazy" and threw me out. Several months later he proclaimed that he couldn't live without me and begged me to come back. Along the way I fell in love with someone new and I had to decide which role to pick – dutiful wife or other woman? Happy or good? I picked happy.

Along the way, I began volunteering at a domestic violence agency after my aunt was murdered by her fiancé. Several years after that I began running one. I ran it until my oldest child was one and the stress of both roles landed me in the hospital with perforating ulcers. I decided to become a full-time mom and frugal housewife. My role changed again.

Over the years, I have been a victim and a survivor, a saint and a slut, an advocate and a basket case. I have been the homewrecker and the long-suffering wife.

Slut Shamed is part of my Poems from the Attic series, poetry that I wrote in my early 20's and then put aside as I got busy earning a living, building a life with my second husband, having children, healing, and otherwise busying myself with a new, healthy life. It is a compilation of poems that deal with issues like sexual abuse, domestic violence, sex and power.

These poems were written in another lifetime. They represent all the parts of who I am and who I was as a woman – victim, temptress, whore, survivor, good little girl and evil vixen. They are also about dozens of other women I have known, loved and mourned.

This book is full of ghosts. One died of a sudden stroke a few years ago. One was killed by her fiancé. One shot herself in the head by Lake Bemidji. One is in hospice right now on the other side of the world, still convinced that she is broken, bad, unlovable. I have learned that life is short for some kinds of girls. I have been those kinds of girls. All of them should still be here today.

It's time to be done with the labels and boxes. We are not saints or whores. We are complicated mixes of everything good and bad. We are fires that light and warm the world. And if you mess with us, it's time to burn it down.

You're So Pretty

E.R.

i lie in the white wired room
flat on my back like always
flocked by men in smocks with
charcoal sludge and epicath
iv's deliver cold wet sugared
life

he enters, king intern
waves them all away like wishes
i am hospital property, he
knows this even though i don't
i pray to him and almost call him
daddy
save me, doctor, stop my bleeding

he is too handsome to be danger
he has your pastor's smile
i swim through consciousness and know
he is protection when he speaks
sedating me with love words
you're too pretty (touch) to kill yourself

and i know i must be crazy when i
feel his hands beneath my shirt
smooth doctor fingers rolling nipples
(you're so pretty)
i wonder if i flash some code then
hurt me i am easy
and i understand their rush to save
this body

DAY LILIES

freckled redheads and bone-pale blondes
clustered in natural bouquets
spreading themselves at the sun
with slippery skin unfolding to please you
tassels of tonsils tickling your eyes

she is a woman made of lips and tongue
of skin made to bloom once
with one day of beauty, no time for grace
straining to outshine
a hundred others on the vine

all for you
all for you

she curls into herself, tucks her soft face
and drops
the wind stirs a thousand sleeping ladies
who have had their day
and who, after all could mourn one flower?
not even a scent remains

UPON WAKING

she cries you know

late at night when you're not listening
or don't want to

we all do
don't ask us why--we've often wondered

but if you ask her in the morning
as she puts on her makeup and scrubs off her dreams
she'll say she never does

ALLOUETTE

Allouette, jaunte allouette, allouette, je te plumerai
Translation: Skylark, yellow skylark, skylark, I am plucking you

Beware the man who wants
to marry you too quickly.
He is as dangerous as Mr. Rogers.
He will want to put you in the pocket of his afghan,
smiling, singing small songs
that sound like French fairy tales.
All the while, through his grin, he will pluck you.

Beware the man who brings you flowers --
you will love him too much.
He will step over you in the doorway,
his Samsonite banging your ribs.
He will come back the moment you forget his birthdate,
grinning, singing French songs. He will pluck you.

Beware the man who wants to make you happy --
he will hate you for it.
At night he'll stick pins in your wishbone,
list his sacrifices on the bathroom mirror.
He will discover that he loved you best suicidal.
Every morning he will pin your smile up,
every evening he will lift your nightgown.

Beware the man who loves you --
he will swallow you whole.

They will all gather with their wide eyes,
licking their lips, and ask for a taste.
They will throw pennies into your mouth,
hoping you swallow. All the while
you'll be gasping for air, repeating "I do, I do."
And when they carry you out at last,
they will lift the sheet, each
wanting to be the last to touch you.

TEN THINGS MY DAUGHTER LEARNED FROM FAIRY TALES

1. Door mats are heroines.

2. Strong women are evil.

3. If you think you are beautiful
   or try to be beautiful, you won't be.

4. If you aren't beautiful, you aren't good.

5. Always listen to men.

6. Never trust women.

7. Clean up after everyone.

8. Marry money.

9. Stay young.

10. Close your eyes.

NOT YOUR USUAL COSMO QUIZ

1. Do you hide yourself in
      1) housework, babywork
      2) outerwork (school, career, social causes)
      3) hunger (drugs, sex, poetry)

2. Do you dream the most of
      1) living
      2) winning
      3) dying

3. Are you everyone's ideal
      1) mother
      2) leader
      3) fuck

4. Do you live the most in
      1) the past
      2) the future
      3) crisis

5. Do you cry
      1) only when nobody else is
      2) only when there's the time
      3) only when awake

Scoring: add up your points, divide by five, round to the nearest number.

See next page.

Ones:

> you raised atlas, you suckle mankind
> you are stronger than all of your sons
> and never will know it
> you feel empty
> and all of the housework, all of the offspring
> can never fill that hole
> you are most afraid
> of breaking down
> there's no one to mother you
> and once, just once, you wish
> someone
> could understand

Twos:

> you are atlas, you dare mankind
> you are stronger than all of the sons
> and want to believe it
> you feel empty
> and all of the projects, all of the triumphs
> can never fill that hole
> you are most afraid
> of resting
> you'd be left alone with yourself
> and once, just once, you wish
> someone
> could understand

Threes:
    you fucked atlas, you tease mankind
    you are stronger than all of his sons
    but no one believes it
    you feel empty
    and all of the parties, all of the tortures
    can never fill that hole
    you are most afraid
    of trying
    you know too much about pain
    and once, just once, you wish
    someone
    could understand

WHITE WALLS

wires on the windows, white on the walls
nobody to give good head to
and all i do
is sit in my sickness and contemplate
the number of ways left to kill
a small blonde with no reason to die.

bright red roses by my bedside, sweet white
wrappings on my wrists.
he's fucking someone else but i
get roses. i'm so clean, so white.

i should be bleeding.

a real person would mind the visits
after midnight by the man in white.
he has no right to white.
white is for crazies, victims,
girls who give good head. white
is so they can see when we bleed.
i close my eyes
and he is nothing but black.

at lunch they shuffle us around
like cards in a stacked hand.
anorexic girls and old old ladies
are wheeled back and forth
in the same halls.
i keep quiet and hide my wrists
till dark, safe in my white box
where i listen all night
but no one ever screams.

white like fangs.
white like bones.
white like skin
that will never see the sun.

at night i write letters to god
on similax stationery
from the nice nurse.
she lets me smoke my long white cigarettes
while i dream of
nothing but white.

SERVICE

It's hard to think with your dick in my mouth
but baby if I did I think I'd
be wondering what I'm doing with you.
You call me up at
2 in the morning, talking about the
need you have
tucked in your Levis
and I sit here wiping the cum off my shoulders
and wondering why I
can't be a lesbian
and knowing you won't like the idea
of holding me close while I tell you my stories.
So I just
grin and put my ass in the air.
Fuck me till I
can't feel my heart beat.

You Know How Women Are

ENTITLED

i wore white to my wedding
but my daddy stood and winked and i
turned brown
but the bridesmaids they wore
red, it showed their bleeding
cuz they bled you know
they weren't all healed like me
and me
i just stood and made promises
to the lord my father who
i can't trust either
cuz i know what daddies do
and i thought
there's new chains now and
this man owns me
you can't rape the
willing so
i'll never say no

and the world turned orange
rice fell like fingernails
i watched the flower girl
tossing petals from
some rose that should
be blooming
and in her eyes i saw
that it had
started too
i howled-- the men
just laughed
you know how women are

PURGED

if they knew
and if they asked me why
i do it
i wouldn't know

maybe i'd say
it's the rush
that comes with the forbidden
my longest finger
sneaking down the cavern
water running so no one hears

maybe it's a
sacrifice
that draws up
the guilts and sins and worries
sucking at my belly

or maybe it's a punishment
denying nourishment
inflicting pain
on this
undeserving body

but i wouldn't say
that it's for you
a last clandestine uprise
(you can't rule me
and you can't make me better)
that i'm in control
no i'd never say that
my love

REFLECTIONS ON HANES

those panty hose ads
i hate em
you know the ones
reflections on laura
who does crossword puzzles
in ink!
who loves hot dogs
and her legs...
we, i suppose
are to marvel at her
individuality
and go buy hanes

but i always think
that's it?
that's the only 2
differences
between laura
and 5 million other
great legged beauties?
and if laura
really does have
such legs
why does she need panty hose
at all
unless she's cold
in which case she'd just wear jeans
or snow boots
because after all
she is an individualist

SHE THINKS SHE'S AN EAGLE

I have two days to learn about spirit animals
so I visit Ruth, who always knew about such things.
Jerry watches the baby for ten minutes
while we smoke a cig on her front steps.

"Some say it's whatever you dream of"
she tells me, stealing a drag of my cigarette,
"I always dream of stallions."
I think of Freud, keep nodding.
"Some say it's what you identify with."
She looks at the suburban starless sky--
"Me, I think I'm an eagle."

Inside the house, Jerry calls for her.
She trots inside,
fetches his sweater.
Oh Ruth, I think,
How sweet you are.

TARAXACUM OFFICINALIS

he said you were his
dandelion
not so fancy, not so rare
not so beautiful
deceptively simple

you left him

you changed your hair color
every season
scattered
and every man you touched
you stained

MASENGILL

limb-lax in class
i noticed
scents of my soul spot
the fog of earth
hissing out

my nose was unoffended
not a flower
not a fruit
but a woman
i smell like a woman
like the rich dark
land that bore me

but a lady
shouldn't stink like one
my legs snapped shut

BATHING THE NUDE SAVIOR

Mary, after all these years of running from religion,
It is your bones I smell. Suddenly
I am filled with questions, not about God
But you.

What became of your body, Madonna? Surely
It was not yours anymore. Like the girl touched
By a movie star, never to wash that arm again
No mere man could enter after that.
Your breasts too, suckling Jesus-- how
Could they accept a husband's touch? Even your hands
Bathing the nude savior, became too clean
For anything else. Only your lips
Remained yours, but what could you do with them?

What became of your body, Madonna?
Did it ever want another savior, just
To come to life again?

OH YES

the car won't start
and i'll do the dishes
there's a check that bounced
and the dog needs walking
and yes--oh yes-- i'm dying here and
your mother called
and i mowed the lawn
and your daughter grew up while you weren't looking
and by the way, i just can't make it

there's a man on the street that said he'd
kill you for seventeen dollars
and i'm thinking, thinking maybe
i'll just get in the car and drive to alaska
and leave your shirts in the bottom of the hamper
cause i'm too tired and i'm too bored to
care anymore if i satisfy you

you said one time that i gave good head and
it got me through the next seven years
but baby i just
need some livin'
and the boss called while you were at work
said you left three hours ago
and i wondered if she
gave good head and
cried when you left there

so put down your beer and look in my eyes
cuz you may not seem 'em for a very long time
and lately i've been thinking, thinking
that i can do better than
this two story house with a bed full of headaches

there's a tv dinner in the microwave
i'll call you when i
get to alaska

And We Never Cry

FLOWERED

did you make love tonight?
was he gentle? has he ever been?
do you ever try to cry?

i still have a photo of you--flowered,
the sign said. you wore your glasses and buck teeth.
deflowered is missing. i prefer the other,
before you tried to be beautiful.

i remember the man who bought you rubies.
i was so impressed. you gave them back
and i could have killed you. integrity
is no match for rubies.

i should never have left. i came back
and you were a married mother, ashamed
of your past.

there are no screams
in a town that small. you smile and go make supper.

i have seen you with the knife in your hand,
your wrist red and your eyes wild.
i have read the old poems, i was there
when you dreamed, and when you told me,
years later,
          i'm so glad it was a boy, girls
          have so much pain.

was he gentle? has he ever been?
do you ever try to cry?

DANCING GIRL

even after you left
the last of my dancing girls
still i kept on with the spinning
spinning   spinning
i was gonna be the one
to bring back your legs girl
where are your jingle bells now?

the last two winters took the last of me
i get to be in your court now
we meet in the bars
taking small sips
going home early
empty as ever

and we watch our movies
and we talk of politics
and we hide in the arms of our
big
strong
safe
men

and we keep on going
and we never cry

tell me you're happy
tell me you love him
tell me you're grown up and hate that old life
tell me whatever
but honey remember
i know how your voice
cracks when you lie

CHANCES

the days go by and I dream of sleeping
the years go by and I count them
one by one, one
chance at a time that's
gone, gone forever and
I'm still here and I'm still crying
maybe, maybe
one more chance and one more day to
write a novel to
make a million to
smile-- oh god why can't I feel
happy, with my
tater twister and room full of memories

and the years go by and the nights they just
crawl on bloody hands from
scrapes with bottles and trying to
dance when I can't make it, stand it
down on my knees with blood on my pants
in my home, my box
of my own dead limbs

and all I've got are these old eyes and
this one line

and the years go by

NIGHTMARES

when i was six years old i woke up
screaming
and mama came and said
hush it's ok baby
you just got someone else's dream

mother, i have your husband in my bed
i never planned on wearing white or
being you but here i am
with that same stale smile and
plate glass stare

how did i manage
to drop so easily
into this used life?
i am not as good at it
i never thought i wanted it

mother, i was never meant to be you
the dishes droop in my hands
the smile keeps stumbling
my legs kick at the sheets while i sleep
trying to run
i wake up screaming
still caught in your dream

MOONCHILD

light up the candles, my pretty thing
it's another year of tricks from the man in the moon
stare at the back of his little bald head
and try to pretend that he's thinking of you

the moon and the stars have forgotten your name
but you remember it, don't you
you memorized everything in those old dreams
and you want to be real again, don't you

don't you, my sweet thing, come midnight and quiet
lie in the sheets with your past on your lips
looking up longingly into the night
that told you so many lies

don't you, come darkness, leave that old lover
lying there thinking you want his wide arms
and dream of the times when the stars were your witness
while you danced to the beat of your heart

and don't you, some midnights, hear yourself breathing
feeling that pulse deep inside
hear the soft echo of some small thing crying
and mourn for all that has died

and do you ever feel alive, my pretty?
do you ever feel alive?

WATERGIRL

oh neesie, my housewife alter
open your second eyelids
rise from the bed one night
join me in the icy water, breathe
underwater--
find your fins, watergirl
down in the green world

come to my side, mrs. evans
one night a year
it's all right to bleed
your heart will make new
and when you cut your thumb with the onions
it will be fresher
to drop into his soup

FASHION STATEMENT

one dress. you had one dress
to wear to school
day after day, like the same smile
pasted on for every one of them.
knowing you, you rarely cried.

how hard it must have been
to crouch and watch them:
your laughing mother
and the neighbor
on your father's side of the bed,
to wear that same dress
the next day to hug your father
while your mother made breakfast,
knowing that nothing
would ever be the same.

how hard, to keep that smile
all these years
for your mother, for your husband
later, climbing back into your bed,
for the town that knew...
wearing their lies
like a dress that no longer fits
but is, after all,
all you have.

THE SCORE

we were an odd set,
each monday night
sliding into funny shoes and acting
as if we cared about bowling.
i got drunk
while lisa charmed the grandmas
and jen tried to make us all happy.
you
never hid a thing.
anger and silence grew in you
like a thick mud.
you astounded me
as you threw yourself towards those pins
and slammed them again and again.

we are still bowling
each monday night.
we all need our nights in warm places.
and those ten little men
go down again and again.

every night he cheats you bowl 200.

DIAMOND POINT

she was fire that always wanted to be water,
drowning herself with her own pain.
she was a small storm that does no damage,
a wind that blows itself out,
an exotic food you too soon tire of.

the trees that night looked like angels
made wrong. the gun was borrowed.
she wore a new shirt, like a convict
who dresses up to turn himself in.
she sang her death to an empty car,
the kids back home with mother.

it took forty minutes to die.
her blood kept her warm,
but still she shivered, wondering
which minute it would be.
she never screamed.
she never had.

Closed Eyes

NECROPHILIA

don't you wanna
know
why she never fought them
for her life for her
virtue

about that june night
at the campsite
her stint as a birthday present
with lani laughing   and listening
outside

bout her crying later
how neese left
with joe to protect her
and joe
taking a dip too

or about the hill with brian larson
 you know you want it
bout how by then she didn't
care

she stopped struggling early
cuz there wasn't anything left
to kill

WITNESS

i saw what you did.
i opened the door, the car light
shining on both of you.
she was a virgin, her only sin
drinking too much to fight well.
after, she bled
for 90 days. she turned yellow
and could not walk
until the doctors finally
said okay and had a look.
they can say what they like, i know
she was only trying
to get you out of her.

INTRUDERS

my friend jenna was afraid
of contraceptive sponges.
what if the string comes off, she
wondered, would that soft white disk
float free forever?
a bubbling chunk to sterilize
some parts of her that shouldn't be.

and then there was the girl in high school
who got carried away with her boyfriend
and a snickers bar--
had to go to emergency some friday night
tell some intern of
that chocolate treat inside.

some things should never be
let loose in the female body.

i've got my own wandering oddities--
memories, like wayward candy bars
through my passages.
tied together once like preschoolers
on a field trip,
some men cut the cord, left them
like mowgli, wolf children to fend for themselves.
now black-cloaked scenes that would
give all the answers
crouch dirty in the darkness, sterilizing
some parts of me that shouldn't be.

A SONG FOR THE OTHER CHILDREN

hush little baby, don't you cry
daddy's gonna visit, by and by
he'll bring you presents and show you love
that almost makes up for the things he does

and if that love makes you feel dirty
if those gifts bring too much hurting
then daddy'll make the pain go away
by telling you all that he does is ok

and if at night you still feel sad
keep it in so he don't get mad
in fifteen years you can run from here
but the shame ain't never gonna disappear

you try to beg and you try to fight
but he keeps on coming, every night
it ain't no use for you to cry
mama's in the bedroom, living her lie

so hush little baby, don't say a word
cuz the neighbors aren't looking and nobody heard
you could scream all night and they'd never hear
cuz nobody wants to interfere

so bite your tongue and close your eyes
daddy's gonna visit, by and by

SURVIVORS

she calls us survivors
says that if we lived then we
survived
she doesn't understand
that we are not like her
full of teeth and missions
that we are not surviving
when we cut and burn and loathe our skins
swallow sin like semen
that we have been dying
one cell at a time
and prefer the honest name of
victim
she doesn't understand
that what we do is not called living

DEPTH

i once compared bree to
a lake, saying that what you saw above
was only a reflection of the rest of us.
everyone scoffed and compared her to fireworks, as if
she were nothing but a loud sparkle
and across the table, bree
smiled and showed me her blue.

nobody ever wanted her to be more
than the party favor, the token oddity,
the quick-witted elf. when she chopped off her hair
it was neither a feminist statement
nor fatigue at all the bullshit--
she was just being cute, they said, why look
even bald she's just adorable.

and when she lay in bed for days, crying
at something she couldn't name, they said
well, you know how bree is. she's always been weird.
as if tears on such a creature could only be
something shallow or artistic.

and when she sobbed for me and all my troubles,
year after year, with the whiskey and cigarettes
and poetry that we ate up like tears,
they said she loved the melodrama.

and when she kept getting drunk at parties
and privately touching my cheek, kissing my lips,
whispering she loved me, i loved her back till it bled,
her long nails like barbed hooks
that sliced me open before she threw me back.

she drowned us both and afterwards
they all swam away, cursing
me for dragging her down.

LAURA MILLER'S EYES

she has bedroom eyes and when
she looks at you
she knows exactly how you'd
kiss her on a sticky summer evening
she walks as though she's practicing
the way she'd slide along you
with her satin sheets and
warm wet mouth
and if she touches you
you know that it's a test to see if
your skin is rough enough or
soft enough to please her
she is alive   sexual
she has power
you know it and it makes you angry

you follow and you wait and one night
you find her
when she isn't being watched
she wiggles even then
somehow you knew she would
you surprise her and you coax her
with a hunter's soothing song
you tell her how she's gonna like it
even though you know she won't
she acts assertive but her
bedroom eyes are showing fear
you push her to the ground and when
she struggles it increases your erection

you see her at the coffee shop
you know in daylight she'd never even
know you
you smile
bigger when you
see she isn't smiling back
she is alone
she isn't talking
in that salty woman-voice
she doesn't
sway or slide or touch the men she passes
she walks as though her knees are bound together
and when she looks at you
you see that she's got
coffin eyes
you grin and want to show her
your erection

THE OUTING

The children watch
while mother winds the muddy tube
up the length of a reed of leg.
They see the careful snap,
the shoe slid in,
buckled.
The red smile appears
where there was only a pale word.

Coats and hats are donned.
They embark on a trip that has no name.

It is a man's home --
taboo
in those days for such a group.
The back room is strange and oddly lit.
When the man says merely
perhaps you'd like to wait in the kitchen
it's more comfortable
the woman exits plainly.

Grandma told the story over 60 years,
one word at a time.
It doesn't exist to her
and the dead get no grudges or guilt.
Still
I picture a day
when my grandmother was something soft and small...
three children holding their bare hands,
a story so needy that it crawled out anyway,
black and white photographs
and rent money.

WHITE FEMALE

last week i walked to the laundromat
worked 38 hours, called my mother
bought a pork roast
had a dream about my brother
watched the rain

it was thursday, it was daylight
he had a gun
i was thinking about my garden
and what to cook for supper and
of you
and then i was gasping
and then i was fighting
and then i was trying
to live

i was summarized last sunday
one sentence

last week i had a name

WINTER

It is January and below zero
and I am warm and living
in suburbia, south of a man
who did not die the night he raped me.
Anger is hard to come by, even thinking of it
seems moot this late in the game.

He pinned me down in summer
where wildflowers, crickets, and kids in jeeps
spread faster up that hillside
than his sick semen or my old fear.
This does not forgive him, nor does the truth
that he was halfway down a long, long line.
But there are too many too hate. I'm tired
of pulling water from a dry well.

Call this peace or death or madness
but it will still be winter.
He will still live on, to the north of me,
and good things will still
spread up that hillside.
Something will live there
past us, into spring.

6 YEARS TRAINING

everything i needed to know about being a woman
i learned in grade school.

keep quiet.

look pretty.

stay in your place.

follow the rules.

be lady-like.

stay clean.

don't tattle.

boys against the girls.

When I Was Under Glass

THE WICKED WOMAN

> *"The dwarfs took pity on him*
> *and gave him the glass Snow White--*
> *its doll's eyes shut forever--*
> *to keep in his far-off castle..."*
>
> --Anne Sexton, "Snow White"

During the journey, someone slipped.
Fate erred.
Death came lodged from my throat.
Your beauty woke.

I wanted to move again,
to change my dress, to cut my hair,
play poker with those seven freaks
who loved me first.

I wanted a name, not a title.
A life perhaps.
To live at least through my childhood
before I sat down as Ms. Charming.

The girl you came home with
was not the one you purchased.
How sad, to find the perfect wife
and have her wake.

Now, it is you who lies silent
and I just lie,
looking towards the woods and knowing
you loved me more
when I was under glass.

TO HEAVEN

with the long gold hair and the round grey eyes
you could almost make her an angel
sculpt her a house of roses
at the gate to heaven
you could record the voice, the looks, the way
she laughs and cure the world
you'd like to, if only she
kept on the white

nude, you'd make her a demon
the dark red lips and form for sin
you'd build her temples from the breastbones of nuns
and one of her smiles would wipe god
from the palm of jesus
you'd kill for her
if only she kept out the lights

yours, you make her a housewife
with laundry and bedsheets, the spread
of the legs and the wings
with occasional worship
and an occasional
sacrifice

OFFER

okay you be my christ and i'll be your daughter
don't you think that we can
make a marriage?
if the roasts are good and my penmanship
is good on
christmas cards and the dog gets walking?

you go to sleep and i'll go to heaven
each thursday night in a
locked up bathroom
don't you think that we can
last a lifetime?

i'll be your whore and you pay the phone bill
just hold me tight one
night in a thousand
and i'll be good and i won't cry
too much so you can
hear the tv

don't you think that
i'd be worth it?

BURNING LOVE

shopping for incense
we stopped at love
love
we joked
does love smell good?
will it kill the cat box odor?
let's fill the house with love
darling
grin

now
there's no room in the air
for words
for looks
for the smoke of incense
and you strike a match
not to jasmine
not to oriental musk
but to that old favorite

burning love
to hide another scent

i don't tell you
but i think
so much for that
at least it kills the cat box odor

THE WAKE

and what did she die of?
they asked my husband
(of boredom)
and he said of suicide
oh really they answered
poor man

no no of boredom!
of starvation of the soul!
of loneliness
i answered
i died
for lack of interaction

but life imitates art
and death imitates life
and no one listened
and so i died again

THE PROBLEM WITH HEROES

you saved me
your harness roped me
pulled me from the
cracked-ice river
dangled me to dry
and now i hang
raggedy ann on a string
waiting for the knife

oh yes my savior
you said i was beautiful
and i knew i was
or wished
and now i wait
for you to say i'm not

you loved me
only enough so i'd love you back
not enough so i'd
love me too
and now i dread
the day neither of us does

you saved me
recycled for another user
for yourself
not me
we women have no power
and now i pray
you cut me loose

ALONE AND DAHLIA

Alone and Dahlia
I reflect
     You've never seen me in this
     Christmas-green robe
     Or making love or
               Cross-stitch
It is another night of anger and
I sit preparing
For the footsteps
     And the penance
         For your love
And as I smoke my cigarette I know
That I don't do laundry
That there's no bank account
For a lifetime of road trips
That we would surely
     Burn too fast and
        Then what
It's been one hour and I miss you

With my heart beating for both of us
I cry blue-green tears you've never seen
     And try to sleep and
        Not to dream

THE RIVER

i guess you could say he raped me then
forcing into that soft spot
as if it were something to own

i remember his smile
the one he wore when he hated me
as if he could somehow tell
that it was you i loved
his fingers were rough
his voice thick
a man drunk on envy or rage
a man who gave up believing

and still i slept
right next to him in the heavy night
like a good wife
like a faithful woman
like a girl who knows how to bleed

in the morning i met you
as always and we drove to the river
watching everything that washes away

DRIVE

i am being torn in two
a blonde wishbone
one man at each wrist
each night i stitch myself up again

today we drove to wisconsin
seven hours on the road, to say we'd gone
our spouses at work
your boss winking like a fluorescent light
i told you i love him
i didn't tell you that i love you more
i think

tonight i will cook him meat loaf
i will make love to him
your ring will catch in his hair
i will swim again, from side to side
wishing i could tear in two

tomorrow i will step back into you
and tell you
drive

So Often So Badly

ALL I WANT

all i want is a warm place
with a smoking section, one small bed of roses,
two men to love me at least half of the time.
a dozen books of poems.
a waist you could wrap
with a garter snake.
good ankles.
oh let's go all the way! world peace,
smooth skin till 80, day-long
orgasms and kisses
that make me forget how to breathe.
a father to rise from his grave
and give up drinking.
newt to go home.
and a poem
to stitch up every hole
that just digs deeper.

ON BEING A WOMAN AND A POET

what it is to be a male poet:

when you are a male poet you write strange poems about little things that
nobody thinks about. and you make them think about them. or you write
about things that everybody thinks about, and you make them wonder if
they've been thinking about something entirely different. if you ever write
about something personal, you write it so impersonally that even you regard
your crises as merely odd.

a sample male poem:

      my uncle john had a blonde mustache
      and lung cancer
      still, when i visited his room
      he'd give me two dollars for a pack of smokes
      i made a dollar
      for every day he lost

what it is to be a female poet:

when you are a female poet, you have two options. you can either write
feminist commentaries, or you can write like a man.

two sample female poems:

a poem for the editor of a female journal--

>   Later that night, the boys came
>   like wild dogs.
>   In places, the building
>   gave, like a great aunt
>   crushing the girls to her bosom.
>   After, of the three deaths, the dean said:
>   They only meant to rape.

a poem for the editor of a male journal--

>   See this poem.

MENTOR
(for Nikky Finney)

once a week we swarmed to the sound
of our own voices. and to enter you--
you, who were taller than all of our poems,
your mahogany bones swaying to the sounds
of our patchwork words.

there is a poem in every inch of you:
the dark vines tied up at your temples,
the way you smelled of coconut and california,
the texture of your strange clothes,
and your words, your beautiful words
that raised us towards the sun.

i remember when i brought you monika.
she praised your green eyes, your strange skin.
monika, who wanted to climb into a white woman's womb,
was proud that day, that she was closer to you
than i.

you taught me
that even a word must earn its respect.
everything was small case to you but Life.
you showed me how to love my tears
and my own mind. and when you left i imagined you
riding your bicycle towards the sun,
poems flying behind you.

RIGHTS

our summer term women's
studies teacher gave
chris a B she said
the paper was great
it's just that chris was
wrong.
today in the poets' market
book i saw a journal say it
wanted anything good but not
sentimental personal haiku
pornographic boring
wrong.
and i keep thinking bout
how in a free country we're
not free to wear a t-shirt
someone else don't like or
go inside a clinic or burn up
a piece of cloth that represents
our freedoms
or live ways they think are
wrong.
i always thought that
feminism poetry freedom
meant you could say and do
and write and fuck and wear
and think
anything and nobody was
wrong.

BEST OF

i have been studying the great
american poets
best of, from '87, '89, '91
the library does not carry
'93. i can only hope
the rules have not changed

i have been studying the women mostly
they have what i want
i notice
the rules are the same as for a man
the whimsical voice of the past
with the strange and the vulgar
of a time when fuck
is said more often than

you. i have learned some lessons:
it is wise, if you are a woman
to write about genitals
male ones mostly, editors love anything
that reminds them of their own testicles
it is also good
to be a man about it
no raw emotion, missy
tell us instead about
shit. or if they are high-brow
a tree stump. a train ride. a bull.
(mention his balls, high-brow or not)

tell us about your mother's death
so we won't miss her
the underwear
they buried her in
the voices she heard
40 years before the cancer
not about your father
screaming at the doctor, but instead
the doctor's tie

that is what it is to be great, i've discovered
to write about things that don't matter
or if they do, to make them not

THE PROCESS

a lady sits here typing
her rose revlon fingers tapping keys
blond and small and nicely shaped
waiting for validation

she's got scars somewhere
from no nice reason
if she had makeup on it'd be too much
she knows it but she does it
anyway
she's better than them but worse than the others
and the others are the only ones that count
she cries a lot but not enough
to get it over with
she's got long eyelashes and pale skin
plus a nineteen inch waist
it'd be sixteen if she exercised
she's got cigar burns for eyelids
and a hole where some man ripped her
and it traveled to her brain

a lady sits here typing
knowing this and thinking this
and wishing for a poem to come
to make her a person

THE PAGE

after weeks of silence, i return to this
the blank god that makes me bleed
and heal, and leave my husbands.
the white lover who always gives back
filling its void with mine,
making something out of nothing
of each of us.

HIGH HOPES

it should console me that today
shakespeare wouldn't be published
that i am the favorite poet
of most of my friends and a local journal
and that even i hate
most of the poems that are published
i can still make em cry, gasp, stammer
and a few of the rejections
have been hand written
but instead it consoles me
that publishers are old men
and old men die
so often so terribly

What You Cannot Own

AUNT LINDA'S GHOST

aunt linda's ghost
sat five hours
warming in the cooling body
she watched her lover
clean the mess
felt her own stiff fingers
as he bent them round the gun
like bald pipe cleaners

she fought death's undertow
trying to reach into one finger
paint his crime on the beige carpet
or at least shake off
his ring

she was there as he dialed
her mother
with trained tears that sounded tortured
heard the story the first time
saw him reach and lift
the heavy thing that killed her first
heard him shuffle down the stairs
to make it gone

she rode with them to the hospital
while grandma consoled him
staring at the van in front
where the rest of her was

once there she heard the doctors say
that she'd been cold too long
those precious organs
were as dead as she
the card she'd signed so hopefully
would give no small person
her pretty pink liver
or proud kidneys

but wait! they said
it's not all wasted
we'll scrape off her skin
scoop out her eyes
and slice those ears away
and those
can still be useful
she can donate those to others

and linda's ghost
always the martyr, agreed
(though truth be told
she no longer had the say)
and off they went

and as they peeled off purple flesh
she thought of lamp shades
and wondered if it would still be
bruised
on the next guy
and would he mind
she apologized the eyes were not
as good as some
but those ears, she said
are quite a prize

(though no one heard, not even linda)

her senses gone
she no longer felt
the pain of his angry hands
could not see his twisted face
or hear the thud
the gunshot
a survivor (well in one sense)
she learned to get around just fine

now aunt linda's ghost
roams the prison
sleeps on the bed by the bloodstains
comes over to our house to
shoot the bull

like venus de milo
like the lady of justice
like a snuff
film actress
with only her tongue
to whisper nights to all of us
how much she gave
for love

WEDDING DAYS

later, alone
he pulls her, pressing
tuxedo to laura ashley gown, releases
the rest of her cleavage, rolls
breasts from hand to hand, like gerbils

gujarat, india
number 1787 dies
a kitchen accident, they say
she pushes the percent to 19
of women's deaths by
such culinary exits
kitchens, it seems
are dangerous in india
especially on wedding days

they leave the presents wrapped, he opens
his bride instead, pushing
into the place he knew but
never owned until today, moaning
as she pictures the beautiful service

supposedly they pour kerosene
on them, then light the girls
like birthday candles
reportedly their dowries
didn't do

later, again
he handles her, wanting
to devour the white body, now
his, knowing
she can't say no, not
this day

                              gujarat, india
                              some mother says goodbye,
                              knowing
                              that these things happen

sometime, she'll open the cards
see words again and again
about wedding days and happiness and
burning love

SEVEN WITH PAROLE

did she scream when you killed her?
did she throw out one last
furied, frightened wail?
(and did it sound the
same as in the movies?)
or did you rather feel
the squishing thud,
the half-cough of
her last breath in?

does a woman's skull make
splinter sounds or
  crack
or does it just collapse?
at such famous moments do you
notice little things like was
she breathing out or in
and did she know?

tell me wayne
with your two small children and
private plane
do you dream about her?
and when you wake are you sorry
because she died
or because she put you there?

every time you cut your finger
nick your face while shaving
do you see how little blood there
is compared to hers?

or do you merely count the seconds
(ticking like her heartbeat)
of those seven years
till you can once again be mister right
and kill
what you cannot own

WITCHES

It is Hecata night, the night to celebrate
Wicca and everything female that is strong.
I am alone. I think it is better.
It is a night to be singular.

Tonight Daryl subbed in pool league. In between
I visited the ladies room and sat
butt to butt with a woman who did not want to be old.
I told her she did not look 50
and she was beautiful when she smiled.

Tonight is the night for witchcraft.
For being strong.

Val is asleep. Like a good mom
I packed her lunch. Tomorrow she will save a woman
from a man who loves her. One of those men
was on Daryl's team. He looked like a batterer
and I pretended not to know his story.
Still he would not look me in the eye. He knows
I volunteer.

A night for women who are not afraid.

The house is still messy. In this small town
I feel I have failed at my only vocation.
My flowers bloom
but the laundry stays undone. We are too far
from a city that says I can be a poet.

I get drunk too often.

There are women who are under the moon tonight.
Women who weave magic.

X did not shoot well.
All the while I knew I could beat him, but women
are not allowed in their league.
He knows I could beat him. I hope. Here
we must take strength where we can.

EMPATHY IN C MINOR

Oh yes, my dear
still yet, my sweet
I am still here.
I am with you
like a god who always forgives,
who always pretends to forgive.

I have fastened your sins into chains
like scars around my heart.
I have swallowed your fist.
I have born your blood.
I have slept in your hate for so long
that without it I feel naked,
like a finger without a ring.

I believe in you.
I believe
in every lie you ever told me.
I know better
in every way that doesn't count.
I believe.
I believe.

After all that you've done, and because of it
I am your small dead plaything,
your crazy girl,
your ugly extra.
I know better.
I know
I should know better.
I'm just so very tired.

Tonight I will crawl in your bed
and hold myself
the way a mother holds a child.
I will pray. I will try to be good.
I will try not to move too quickly,
take too much,
or dream.

BUTCHERED

we are the kind of women
who will never be friends
i would dance for her
bleed for her
i would take her in my mouth and
suck the poison
i will not lie for her
she will not wake for me

yet still i watch her still i
cry sometimes at night for
her and what is coming

i watch her work
see how proudly
she lines the chickens on the skewers
they pose and swell for their mistress
sweat running with the spices down their legs
her artwork

my eyes are on her as
she makes a meal of sacrifice
for him
the meat man she will marry
she speaks the chant
oh honey i'm so dumb and you will be my
savior
as he gets thick with power

and i know her only dream is that
she'll live and that
is something to her
see the tall white house
and three plump children
amy's paradise

and i see her in the bathroom every
sunday night
mama where's my heart and when
can i be happy?
see her crying as she
lifts her nightgown
bleeds for him

at the deli amy's chickens
proudly turn and glisten
and burn
in their small glass prison

DOMESTIC ABUSE

oh, for the sweet stale smell of it!
those polite words are on your graves.
like a flaw in the marriage, a speck of an error,
an "oops" when a husband misbehaves.

and what else to call it? it's not like it's murder.
this is an accident, this isn't planned.
like a push after supper, a nudge toward the bedroom,
this is just love that got out of hand.

this year in florida a man was arrested
for shooting his unfaithful wife.
she'd cheated before, he got 17 months
and then he'll go on with his life.

all over the country, all over the world,
"domestic abuse" is treated politely.
thousands are dying each day, but still
the men have their reasons. we punish it lightly.

let's cut the crap, guys. let's name it right.
let's call it clubbed to death, shot in the head.
let's say the words: she was killed by her husband.
let's print she bled to death, on her own bed.

domestic abuse is such a nice phrase
but if you don't call it murder, you're lying.
stabbed, shot, beaten and strangled:
these are not domestic ways of dying.

Those Evil Bitches

KOHL

she wears revenge instead of eyeliner.
she comes back, daily, to pick up
a pair of shoes, some jam, her life.
she says he is not to blame, i am,
for letting him.   she thinks
if she stays long enough, he'll forget
that he left her.
i
could care less about her revenge,
i wear her eyeliner. she has a lot to learn
about making up.

HEDONISM

i am the homewrecker
i am the anti-christ
i am the salty fluid that you spit
from pinched episcopalian lips
it is so easy
i wear my black so well

the cross suits you
arms open in your clean pressed pain
legs shut against the other pain
the only part of marriage
that you'd let me take away
you wear your white so well

and yes, they will pray for you
and pray for him
that he might break the spell
between my legs
but never for me
i am beyond salvation

forgive me
for loving your husband
more than my neighbor
for loving myself more than you
(i make a lousy martyr)
for feeling the twitch
within my thighs
and liking it
for being strong and being honest
and for being your husband's
equal

yes, i am the sinner
the other woman
the slut who doesn't know her
place with men
(and husbands)
the devil, if you will

but honey
don't forget what
else i am--
the victor

BLOOD LETTING

yes, i have tasted his blood
it was an evening of passion
and a small cut on the neck
there was not enough to tell
his blood type or rh factor
put your crosses back--i am
no vampire, only showing him
that he is in my blood

AMPU- TATIONS

i am a
chamele
on thick
skinned
cold
blooded
unre
liable
to survive
cut off my tail i grow
an other
it will
change too
last month
i loved
you now the land is white
i am pure
again
sorry
to
leave
you
so
alone
in b
l
a
c
k

BOUND

how strange to have this life
within me
       this casserole of his and my cells
           a cocktail of his and my blood
               an omelet without breaking the egg
how odd that soon it will have
a heartbeat later a brain wave someday
       first tooth first car first
          love and all because
one night i crawled into bed
with red lipstick and his
best tie

how strange to think that
a blue dot and sore nipples could morph into
       eternity
and all because one night
       we only thought of the moment and
          i wanted to be
tied down

KANGAROO MOTHER

> A mother kangaroo, when chased
> will dump her young so that she can escape.

At first they kept slipping,
jumping.
I couldn't keep them for all the turbulence.
I'd turn back too late
then keep running.
Later they learned to hold on better.
I would try, really,
the weight of their need in my belly,
poverty closing in on us,
suburbia biting at my heels.

I had somewhere I was going.
My pockets were so full already
of therapy, poetry, plans
and so much of me had been lost
in other battles.
I could sacrifice them
or all of us.

From their safe televisions
mothers everywhere condemn me.
Perhaps they don't understand
or maybe they do, too well.
I pay little attention.
Until I can stop running
I don't have the luxury
of looking back.

AZUCAR

Be wary, Nicholas, she is not what she seems.
Rich girl gone bad, bad girl dressed good,
She hasn't decided on
Which role.
I have seen her, in every photograph,
With either a beer or a man.
Cosmo woman with a war wound,
She will look to you to save her
Or to pay for her.
Step lightly.
Remember, Nicholas--
To the rich and the strong, everything
Is disposable.

EVER AFTER

it is twenty
years later. snow white,
as she is still known,
is thirty-two. she sees
the pleating of the skin
around her eyes, the droop
of his favorite breasts,
the bumps beneath
what was always firm. she sits
in front of an old mirror,
inherited from a woman once young.

in the next kingdom, cinderella
has cast off her slippers.
her feet, swollen from pregnancies and winters,
are constant reminders of
what no longer fits.

briar rose takes prozac
but still cannot sleep without fear
of who she'll wake up to,
who she'll wake up as.

the princes, with their little pot bellies
are eying each other's daughters

and the queens
those nasty bitches
just laugh and laugh.

ESCAPISM

Flipping through
      Glamour
I see an ad
Escape For Men

Awful spendy shit

But I wire calvin
Make it
Escape From Men
And you've got a deal

Whether To Dream

MOON RUNNING

it's me again
sitting here trying to
live or die or reconcile
the two sides of my heart
not really doing much
breathing a little
feeling a little
trying to decide
whether to dream
and of course
about what

last night i rode
through the empty parts of minnesota
topless
standing into the wind
throwing my breasts out the window
and trying to blow out my heart
or force air back into my lungs
or maybe wake up
and today my breasts are beautiful
and miss the night

you say you're holding me back
but you were the one driving
and i wonder how long you could last
being the clothed one
i wonder if nudity gets old and
whether eventually
we'd just crash

IRISES

Maybe you hate irises
because your mother loved them --
those slim and delicate ladies
that required no care, blooming
out on their own, every year
after the Minnesota cold.

Maybe your mother loved them
for that paradoxical beauty --
fragile, ethereal flowers
on a plant that would take anything
or nothing, from her
and still grow strong.

Now in your own garden
are moss roses, cosmos, zinnias,
geraniums that you carefully tend
and bring inside to warm in winter.
I watch you weed them, water them
while your mother drinks whiskey
and lets the irises roam.

And Cindy, your flowers are beautiful
and strong
but your mother's slender blooms are just
as magic, growing still
despite her, with constant
brave and stunning beauty.

SILVER

for twenty years she wore that bracelet
like a price tag never removed.
you scolded her from the time
you learned about fashion. it was taboo.
it was silver once, plated.
it aged faster than your mother,
marred her. chipped copper, cheap metal
defacing the slender bare skin used to gold.
you and your brothers bought new ones.
your father smiled, lovingly,
at his crazy wife. for twenty years
you turned your eyes from the symbol,
never wrapped it in your fingers, never saw
the faint white chains beneath the band, scars
from when your mother was marred too.
you never learned about the year before you,
when your father left and your mother
tried to. you never knew
she liked it
better than he did, and tried to stay
with a new man who loved her in silver.

SAINT JOSEPH'S

saint joseph's hospital
sits on harrodsburg road, looking
too friendly for my liking
not white and crisp like it's
insides
but homey, like
some new large church
to visit christmas eve

there's a man in there
he works with joy
or rather she works for him
he has a rolodex of women
raped in childhood
   doctor i keep crying
   why can't i let my husband
   touch me
   i keep seeing those eyes
   and my daddy's cock
he could uncap my head
ease out the memories
for ninety-two fifty an hour

the emergency room
is always tidy
and in my mind is always empty
like that night with
no one screaming but my mother
i remember how many beds it had
i had to walk so far to see her
though i could hear her in the waiting room
three days later they operated

emergency brain surgery
        don't worry
        it's ninety-nine percent effective
my mother was never lucky
she's dying again

i pass saint joseph's
on the back of michael's motorcycle
always drawn to look
at the neat brick building
picture some man at a desk
sending in each incest survivor
like changing the channel
see my mother's cloroxed bed
and wonder who is dying in it

saint joseph's makes me angry
offering so much hope
to hopeless people
the lottery with the biggest jackpot
but like the woman selling food stamps
for a ticket
i keep returning, hoping
some young intern can undo the wrongs
of god and men
and sell some life

ONE GAME

the early spring air cracks
with the weight of morning
as cindy smokes
just one more cigarette
and plays just one more game

the mouse clicks in her anxious hand
    just one more time
    i know
    i can win

somewhere in the country
he is rising from the couch
cindy clicks on
while jen and i read tarot cards
and sing love songs like we mean em

by now he is shuffling to the shower
his wife is spitting through the walls

i go downstairs and check on cindy
whose eyes are fresh with dew
she asks me if i think he'll do it
after promising so many times

he drives off to work
the papers safe in his glove box
wondering if he can do it
after failing her so many times

soon it will be time
to get the kids off to school
cindy says she'll quit
as soon as she wins
just once

NOTHING WAS WASTED

and if the ghosts of
fathers, rapists, rooms full of lawyers
should claim me while i
sleep tonight
then don't you cry and don't you
feel like
something was wasted
cause i had some friends and a really good time
with wine coolers and some guys in black
and i wrote some poems and i made some stories
and i lived a lot
longer than most girls

SOMEDAY

someday she will speak again
twenty years from monday
a bone
directly left of her wishbone
will break in two and
she will spill out
right past the dirty dishes
over the burnt stew
past the bedroom
up the driveway
into herself

we will all be there
out of our collective comas
singing

and i will love her wrinkles
and i will love her freckled breasts
and i will love her fresh full soul

and she will love her voice

it is waiting
twenty years from monday
she will wake up god

THE PRINCE

and oh, she was beautiful
that porcelain prop
that pristine treat
that sweet dumb thing
who tasted white on my lips

when i gave her breath
she was so grateful
i thought i would love her forever

but now
with her high dreams
with her goals and ideals
of saving my kingdom
treating my women
like more than witches or queens
i sneak into her room and watch her sleep
but she always wakes on her own

and i
i have grown into
something to wear on her arm
not a savior but a useless man
who only knows how to kiss

her sweet dumb thing
i fill her room with apples
but she has grown too wise

ABOUT THE AUTHOR

Alicia Bayer lives in small Minnesota town with her husband and five children. She is the author of seven books and her writing has been featured widely in magazines and online. She and her family run a community arts center out of a historic church they bought for the price of a used car.

OTHER BOOKS BY ALICIA BAYER
IN THE *POETRY FROM THE ATTIC* SERIES:

Crazy Broken Thing
Cradle and All (Coming in 2023)

OTHER BOOKS BY ALICIA BAYER

Poems from Under a Toadstool
A Magical Homeschool: Nature Studies
Elderberries: The Beginner's Guide
Acorn Foraging
Getting Started Homeschooling